EGGLESS
RECIPES
100%
Vegetarian

The Chocolate Cook Book

TARLA DALAL

India's #1 Cookery Author

S&C

SANJAY & CO.
BOMBAY

Sixth Printing 2006

Copyright © Sanjay & Company

ISBN No. 81-86469-34-6

Price : **Rs. 230/-**

Published & Distributed by :

SANJAY & COMPANY,

353/A-1, Shah & Nahar Industrial Estate, Dhanraj Mill Compound,

Lower Parel (W), Mumbai - 400 013. INDIA. Tel. : (91-22) 2496 8068.

Fax : (91-22) 2496 5876 E-mail : sanjay@tarladalal.com

❖

**Research &
Production Design**

PINKY CHANDAN

ARATI KAMAT

JYOTI SHROFF

❖

Designed by

S. KISHOR

❖

Photography

VINAY MAHIDHAR

❖

Food Styling

NITIN TANDON

❖

Printed by

MINAL SALES AGENCIES, Mumbai

OTHER BOOKS
BY TARLA DALAL

INDIAN COOKING
Tava Cooking
Rotis & Subzis
Desi Khana
The Complete Gujarati Cook Book
Mithai
Chaat
Achaar aur Parathe
The Rajasthani Cookbook
Swadisht Subzian

WESTERN COOKING
The Complete Italian Cookbook
Eggless Desserts
Mocktails & Snacks
Soups & Salads
Mexican Cooking
Easy Gourmet Cooking
Sizzlers & Barbeques
Chinese Cooking
Easy Chinese Cooking
Thai Cooking

TOTAL HEALTH
Low Calorie Healthy Cooking
Pregnancy Cookbook
Baby and Toddler Cookbook
Cooking with 1 Teaspoon of Oil
Home Remedies
Delicious Diabetic Recipes
Fast Foods Made Healthy
Healthy Soups & Salads
Healthy Breakfast
Calcium Rich Recipes
Healthy Heart Cook Book
Forever Young Diet
Healthy Snacks
Iron Rich Recipes
Healthy Juices
Low Cholesterol Recipes
Good Food for Diabetes
Healthy Subzis
Healthy Snacks for Kids
High Blood Pressure Cook Book
Low Calorie Sweets [New]
Nutritious Recipes for Pregnancy [New]

GENERAL COOKING
Exciting Vegetarian Cooking
Entertaining
Microwave Recipes
Quick & Easy Cooking
Saatvik Khana
Mixer Cook Book
The Pleasures of Vegetarian Cooking
The Delights of Vegetarian Cooking
The Joys of Vegetarian Cooking
Cooking With Kids
Snacks Under 10 Minutes
Ice-Cream & Frozen Desserts
Desserts Under 10 Minutes
Microwave Snacks & Desserts

MINI SERIES
A new world of Idlis & Dosas
Cooking Under 10 Minutes
Pizzas and Pastas
Fun Food for Children
Roz Ka Khana
Microwave - Desi Khana
T.V. Meals
Paneer
Parathas
Chawal
Dals
Sandwiches
Quick Cooking
Curries & Kadhis
Chinese Recipes
Jain Desi Khana
7 Dinner Menus
Jain International Recipes
Punjabi Subzis
Corn
Microwave Subzis [New]

INTRODUCTION

Rich, creamy, soft, sumptuous, indulgent are just a few of the words that spring to mind when you think of CHOCOLATE.

The enchantment of chocolate has grown over the years, thanks to the ingenuity of today's chocolate manufacturers. The selection of chocolate products available is overwhelming. Just to list a few, dark chocolate, milk chocolate, white chocolate, chocolate chips, chocolate vermicelli, apart from the large array of ready-made chocolate confections.

You can spend several indulgent hours in the kitchen creating that perfect extravagant gateâu or pop into the kitchen to rustle up a cake or a batch of cookies for afternoon tea.

There is nothing quite as nice as home-made chocolates. There is a special charm in presenting fresh home-made chocolates which are not only cheaper but also healthier since the freshest and the best quality of ingredients available would naturally be used.

Working with chocolate can be fun, but let me warn you that it can be a bit frustrating for a beginner. Like most hobbies, although it may be difficult at first, it is rewarding when you see that you have created something beautiful.

There is no magic formula except to keep trying patiently and to follow all the instructions carefully. You will be pleasantly surprised with the results.

HAPPY COOKING !

Tarla Dalal

Cocoa and chocolate are both derived from the cocoa bean which grows in pods on the cocoa tree.

The cocoa tree originated in the Amazon forests but now grows as far apart as West Africa and Malaya.

When the cocoa pods are harvested, the pulp and cocoa beans are scooped out and allowed to ferment. Fermentation is a vital stage in the cocoa and chocolate making process. It develops the chocolate flavour as we know it by removing the astringency of the unfermented bean. After this process, the wet mass of beans is dried, usually by being spread out in the sun.

1. The dried cocoa beans are then sorted and cleaned. The beans are then roasted in revolving drums. It is through this roasting that the bean takes on its characteristic flavour and aroma and the shell becomes brittle.

2. These roasted beans are then broken down into small fragments and the brittle shell is separated. These small fragrant beans are called "nibs".

3. The nibs are then ground between steel rollers until the friction and heat of milling gradually reduces it to a thick, dark brown coloured liquid called "Chocolate Liquor". This contains 55% cocoa butter. The mixture is also called "mass" and solidifies on cooling.

This "mass" is the basis of all chocolate and cocoa products. Cocoa is made by extracting some of the cocoa butter from the cocoa mass. Chocolate is made by adding extra cocoa butter and sugar to the ground nibs. In the manufacture of milk chocolate, milk is also added.

Chocolate is a high calorie food product and its quality depends on the quality of raw materials used and the care taken during its stages of manufacture. **A good chocolate is shiny brown, breaks cleanly and is free of lumps, tiny burst bubbles and white specks. It melts on the tongue and is neither greasy nor sticky.**

Chocolate is extensively used in confectionery for numerous cakes, desserts, frosting, sauces etc. It is also used for some lesser known savouries, e.g. the unsweetened variety is used in Mexican cooking.

CHOOSING AND STORING CHOCOLATE

Before buying chocolate, check the recipe and use what the recipe calls for. It is best to keep chocolate wrapped in foil or plastic. Here are a few golden rules of storing chocolate.

1. Always store chocolate in a cool, dry place away from direct heat or sunlight.
2. Chocolate can be refrigerated in summer, but it is necessary to bring it to room temperature before chopping or grating. Sometimes chocolate will develop a white "bloom" on its surface. This is usually a result of a change in the sugar chemistry or a radical change in temperature. However the bloom is harmless and does not affect its flavour but keep in mind that stale chocolate (which can also develop a bloom) is unpleasant and dry and should not be used.

HOW TO MELT CHOCOLATE

As chocolate is very sensitive to heat, the aim is to melt the chocolate uniformly without cooking it or burning it.

1. Chocolate from a bar or block should be chopped or grated for uniform melting.

2. Place the chocolate pieces in a heatproof bowl and then stand this bowl over a pan of gently simmering water. Make sure that the base of the bowl is not in contact with the water and that the water is **not boiling** rapidly. This is called a **DOUBLE BOILER.**

3. Stir continuously until the chocolate has melted and the mixture is smooth.

Try to prevent any water or steam coming into contact with the melted chocolate. A small amount of liquid, even from a wet spoon may cause the chocolate to seize and stiffen, rendering it unusable.

Also bear in mind that the weather will affect the melting and re-setting times of chocolate. Try not to expose the chocolate to extremes of temperature.

Once you have mastered the art of melting chocolate, working with chocolate will be a satisfying experience.

WHICH CHOCOLATE SHOULD YOU USE ?

PLAIN CHOCOLATE / DARK CHOCOLATE

It has a slightly sweet flavour and a dark brown colour. Plain chocolate can contain anything from 30% to 75% cocoa solids. It is the chocolate used mostly in cooking and confectionery.

MILK CHOCOLATE

As its name suggests, it contains milk and has a creamy, mild and sweet flavour. It is light brown in colour and is mostly used as eating chocolate rather than in cooking. It is good for decorations but care is required while melting it as it is sensitive to heat.

WHITE CHOCOLATE

Technically, white chocolate is not chocolate at all because it contains no chocolate liquor. It is a commercial product made from cocoa butter, milk and sugar. White chocolate has recently become very popular and is used in mousses, cakes and sauces and as a contrast to other chocolates. As with milk chocolate, **it is sensitive to heat, so be very careful when melting it.**

CHOCOLATE CHIPS

Chocolate chips were originally produced by manufacturers for use in chocolate chip cookies. These are small pieces of chocolate available in 3 varieties, i.e. bitter sweet, semi-sweet and white. Because they are designed to keep their shape in a variety of baked goods, they are best used in recipes like cookies, cakes and confections. Although they can be melted, they contain less cocoa butter than ordinary chocolate and do not melt to form a smooth sauce.

CHOCOLATE VERMICELLI

It is available as dark, white and coloured vermicelli and is used for baking and decoration.

COCOA POWDER

Cocoa is the pure chocolate mass which is left when the cocoa butter has been removed from the chocolate liquor. Ground and sifted, cocoa gives the most intense chocolate flavour to baked goods and desserts.

CHOCOLATE POWDER

Also known as drinking chocolate, this powder is made from cocoa to which sugar and sometimes dried milk solids have been added.

CHOCOLATE SPREADS

These are made mainly from sugar, vegetable oil and flavourings and have a thick but spreadable consistency and can be used as a spread and as dessert toppings. These are also flavoured with hazelnut, nougat etc.

 # WHAT IS CHOCOLATE TRUFFLE AND GANACHE?

Chocolate truffle or ganache is a flavoured cream or frosting made with chocolate and fresh cream and is used to decorate desserts, to fill cakes or sweets and make petit fours.

Chocolate petit four truffles are made of chocolate and cream, then flavoured with rum, brandy, whisky, coffee or nuts and shaped into balls which are coated with chocolate or cocoa powder etc. They are a good accompaniment to coffee at the end of a meal.

DECORATING WITH CHOCOLATE

Chocolate garnishes are extensively used and easy to make. Here are a few easy garnishes. Use tempered chocolate (recipe on page 70) for making chocolate scrolls, shapes, drizzles and leaves.

GRATED CHOCOLATE

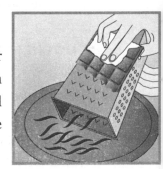

Chill the chocolate and hold it with a piece of folded paper towel to prevent the heat of your hand melting it. Hold a grater over a large plate or a sheet of butter paper and grate the chocolate over it. Use as required. It is advisable not to handle this chocolate with your hands.

CHOCOLATE CURLS

Bring a thick piece or bar of chocolate to room temperature (chocolate which is too warm will slice and that which is too cold will grate). To make the curls, use a sharp knife or a vegetable peeler firmly along the edge of the chocolate to produce long or short curls. Use a skewer or toothpick to transfer the curls to the dessert or cake you wish to garnish. (refer to picture of Mocha Mousse Cake, page 36)

CHOCOLATE SCROLLS (CIGARETTES)

Melt the chocolate and pour in a thin layer of 2 mm. (1/12") on a clean stone or a marble surface. Allow to set until just firm. Place a sharp knife on the surface of the chocolate at an angle of 45°. Pull it gently over the surface of the chocolate to form scrolls. The cooler the chocolate, the more will it splinter. Warm chocolate will give a softer, looser curl but if the chocolate is too warm, it is very difficult to handle.

CHOCOLATE SHAPES

Melt the chocolate and spread a thin layer onto a sheet of butter paper. Allow to cool until firm. Using a cookie cutter or a sharp knife, cut into various shapes like triangles, squares, circles etc.

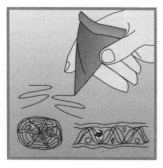

RANDOM SHAPES (DRIZZLE)

Melt the chocolate and pour into a paper piping bag (diagram on page 12). Cut the tip and make designs of your choice on a butter paper.

CHOCOLATE LEAVES

Wash and dry thoroughly any fresh leaf with distinct veins and a good shape such as rose leaf, bay leaf etc. Melt the chocolate and using a pastry brush or spoon, coat the veined side of the leaf. Place these leaves, chocolate side up on a butter paper. Cool till firm and then gently peel away the leaf starting at the stem.

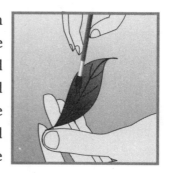

HOW TO MAKE
A PAPER PIPING BAG

1. Cut a 250 mm. (10") square out of grease-proof paper.
2. Fold in half diagonally to form a triangle.
3. Working with the long side facing away from you, pull one corner into the centre.
4. Hold in place while bending in the other corner and wrapping tightly to form a cone shape.
5. Tuck upstanding ends inside the paper cone and fold down to secure. Spoon the melted chocolate into the bag. Fold down bag to seal. Snip off the tip gently and apply pressure to pipe out contents. Practice will make you perfect.

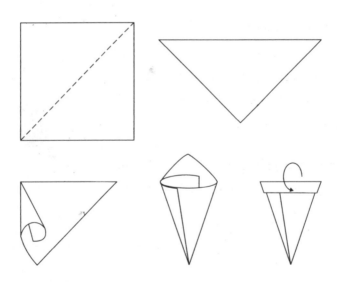

INDEX

COOKIES AND SLICES

CHOCOLATE MAKING

BASIC RECIPES

MANGO TRUFFLE CAKE

Picture on facing page

**A rich chocolate cake layered with
dark chocolate icing and mangoes.**

Prep. time : 15 mins.   Cooking time : 30 mins.   Makes 1 cake.

For the chocolate cake

2 tablespoons cocoa powder

1 cup plain flour (maida)

1 teaspoon baking powder

½ teaspoon soda bi-carbonate

½ can (400 grams for full can)
condensed milk

½ cup melted butter

1 teaspoon vanilla essence

For the truffle icing

2 cups (250 grams)
dark chocolate, chopped

1 cup (200 grams) cream

For the filling

1 mango, peeled and
finely chopped

For the garnish

1 mango, peeled and sliced

8 to 10 red cherries

a few mint leaves

¼ cup fresh cream, whipped

chocolate cream wafer
biscuit rolls (optional)

To be mixed into
a soaking syrup

2 tablespoons sugar

1 tablespoon rum (optional)

½ cup water

Facing page: Mango Truffle Cake, *above*.

16

For the chocolate cake

1. Sift the cocoa powder, flour, baking powder and soda bi-carbonate.
2. Combine all the ingredients together with ½ cup (100 ml.) of water in a bowl and mix well using a whisk.
3. Pour this mixture into a greased 150 mm. (6") diameter baking tin.
4. Bake in a pre-heated oven at 180°C (360°F) for 20 minutes or till a knife inserted into the cake comes out clean.
5. Unmould and cool on a wire rack.

For the truffle icing

1. Put the cream in a saucepan and bring it to a boil. Remove from the flame.
2. Add the chopped chocolate and mix well using a whisk till it becomes a smooth sauce.
3. Cool completely and keep aside.

How to proceed

1. Slice the chocolate cake horizontally into two equal parts.
2. Place the top half of the cake on a serving plate and soak with half the soaking syrup.
3. Spread a generous layer of the truffle icing and the chopped mango.
4. Sandwich with the other half of the cake and soak this half with the remaining soaking syrup.
5. Spread another layer of the truffle icing on top.
6. Cover the sides of the cake with the chocolate cream wafer biscuit rolls.
7. Decorate with swirls of whipped cream, mango slices, cherries and mint leaves.
8. Chill for at least 2 hours before serving.

Facing page: Fruit and Chocolate Gateâu, *page 20.*

FRUIT AND CHOCOLATE GATEÂU

Picture on page 18

Chocolate cake interlaced with seasonal fruits and Chantilly cream makes a sumptuous dessert.

Prep. time : 15 mins.   Cooking time : 30 mins.   Makes 1 gateâu.

1 recipe chocolate cake, page 16

For the Chantilly cream
1¼ cups (250 grams)
fresh cream, chilled

4 tablespoons powdered sugar
1 teaspoon vanilla essence

To be mixed into a soaking syrup
2 tablespoons sugar
2 tablespoons fruit juice
½ cup water

For the filling
1½ cups seasonal fruits (apples, melon scoops, cherries, kiwis, strawberries, peaches, mangoes etc.)

For the garnish
dark chocolate curls, page 10

For the Chantilly cream
1. Combine the cream, sugar and vanilla essence in a clean and dry bowl and whisk till soft peaks form.
2. Keep refrigerated till required.

How to proceed
1. Slice the chocolate cake horizontally into 3 equal parts.
2. Soak the bottom layer of the chocolate cake with the soaking syrup.
3. Spread ⅓ of the Chantilly cream on the soaked layer of the cake.

4. Place ½ cup of fruit on top and sandwich with the second layer of the chocolate cake.

5. Soak with the soaking syrup and spread ⅓ of the Chantilly cream on the soaked layer of the cake.

6. Top with ½ cup of the fruit and sandwich with the third layer of the chocolate cake.

7. Soak with the remaining soaking syrup and spread the remaining Chantilly cream on top.

8. Garnish with the remaining fruit and chocolate curls and refrigerate. Serve chilled.

 CHOCOLATE TIRAMISU TART

An adapted version of the classic Italian dessert.

Prep. time : 30 mins.   Cooking time : 20 mins.   Makes 1 tart.

For the pastry base
½ cup plain flour (maida)

¼ cup butter, frozen and cut into small pieces

1 to 2 tablespoons cold milk

For the chocolate sauce
¼ cup (50 grams) fresh cream

2 teaspoons golden syrup

¼ cup (30 grams) dark chocolate, chopped

For the Coffee Cream Cheese Layer
½ recipe cream cheese, page 86

½ cup (100 grams) fresh cream

2 tablespoons icing sugar

¼ cup (30 grams) milk chocolate, grated

1 tablespoon instant coffee powder
(dissolved in 1 tablespoon hot water)

For the pastry base

1. Sieve the flour into a bowl.
2. Rub the butter into the flour with your fingertips till it resembles bread crumbs .
3. Gradually, add enough cold milk to make a firm dough. Refrigerate for 10 to 15 minutes.
4. Lightly flour the rolling pin and the pastry board.
5. Roll out the pastry to line a 150 mm. (6") diameter tart mould as shown in the diagram on page 48.
6. Prick with a fork at regular intervals.
7. Bake in a pre-heated oven at 230°C (450°F) for 10 to 15 minutes or till golden brown.
8. Cool completely.

For the chocolate sauce

1. Put the cream and golden syrup in a saucepan and bring it to a boil.
2. Remove from the fire, add the chocolate and mix well to get a smooth sauce.
3. Keep aside.

For the Coffee Cream Cheese Layer

1. Whip the cream with the icing sugar till soft peaks form.
2. Mix the cream cheese, milk chocolate and coffee together.
3. Fold in the whipped cream.

How to proceed

1. Spread the chocolate sauce over the prepared pastry base.
2. Top with the coffee cream cheese mixture and refrigerate. Serve chilled.

WHITE CHOCOLATE PISTACHIO PIE

Picture on page 54

**A coconut flavoured chocolate crust topped with a
delicious, creamy white chocolate and pistachio filling.**

Prep. time : 10 mins.   Cooking time : 35 mins.   Makes 1 pie.

For the crust

3 tablespoons butter, softened

3 tablespoons castor sugar

½ teaspoon vanilla essence

1/3 cup desiccated coconut

2 tablespoons cocoa powder

½ cup plain flour (maida)

2 tablespoons cold milk

For the filling

½ cup (60 grams)
white chocolate, grated

½ cup milk

2 tablespoons cornflour

2 tablespoons sugar

½ cup (100 grams)
fresh cream, chilled

For the garnish

2 tablespoons chopped pistachios

whipped cream

fresh fruits, sliced (kiwis, plums, strawberries or mangoes)

For the crust

1. Cream the butter, sugar and vanilla essence in a bowl till light and
   fluffy.

2. Add the desiccated coconut, cocoa powder and flour and mix well.

3. Add the milk and knead gently to make a soft dough.

4. Lightly flour the rolling pin and the pastry board.

5. Roll out the pastry to line a 150 mm. (6") diameter tart mould as
   shown in the diagram on page 48.

6. Prick with a fork at regular intervals.
7. Bake in a pre-heated oven at 180°C (360°F) for 20 to 25 minutes until golden brown.
8. Remove from the oven and cool completely.

For the filling

1. Combine the white chocolate, milk, cornflour and sugar and mix well.
2. Simmer over gentle heat for 2 to 3 minutes, stirring continuously to get a smooth sauce.
3. Cool completely.
4. Whisk the fresh cream in another bowl till soft peaks form.
5. Gently combine the cooled white chocolate mixture and whipped cream using a spatula.

How to proceed

1. Pour the filling mixture over the baked crust.
2. Garnish with the pistachios, whipped cream and fresh fruits.
3. Refrigerate for 4 to 6 hours.
   Serve chilled.

CHOCOLATE MOUSSE

Picture on page 35

A delicious, elegant no-fuss dessert.

Prep. time : 10 mins.   Cooking time : 5 mins.   Serves 4.

2 cups (250 grams) dark chocolate, chopped
1½ tablespoons golden syrup
1½ tablespoons rum
1 cup (200 grams) fresh cream

1. Combine the chocolate, golden syrup and rum in a saucepan and melt over gentle heat till it becomes a smooth sauce. Cool slightly.
2. Whip the cream till soft peaks form and fold it into the chocolate mixture.
3. Pour this mixture into 4 long stemmed glasses.
4. Refrigerate for 4 to 6 hours or till the mousse has set. Serve chilled.

LAYERED CHOCOLATE
MOUSSE CAKE

A sinfully rich chocolate mousse cake.
A milk chocolate and wafer cream biscuit
base topped with a dark chocolate ganache.

Prep. time : 15 mins.　　Cooking time : 5 mins.　　Makes 1 cake.

For the milk chocolate layer

¾ cup (90 grams) milk chocolate, grated

⅓ cup peanut butter

¼ cup Bailey's Irish cream (optional)

½ cup crushed chocolate wafer cream biscuits

oil for greasing

For the dark chocolate layer

1¼ cups (150 grams) dark chocolate, grated

½ cup (100 grams) fresh cream, chilled

For the milk chocolate layer

1. Grease the insides of a 150 mm. x 150 mm. (6" x 6") square cake tin with oil and line the insides neatly with plastic film (You can also use a loose bottomed cake tin).

2. Melt the milk chocolate and peanut butter over gentle heat till it becomes a smooth mixture.

3. Add the Bailey's Irish cream and chocolate wafer cream biscuits into the melted chocolate mixture and mix.

4. Press the mixture into the greased and lined cake tin and refrigerate till it is firm.

For the dark chocolate layer

1. Whip the cream until soft peaks form and keep refrigerated.
2. Melt the dark chocolate over gentle heat and fold it into the cream.
3. Keep aside.

How to proceed

1. Pour the dark chocolate mixture over the set milk chocolate layer.
2. Allow it to set in the refrigerator.
3. Unmould the mousse cake and place on a serving plate. Serve chilled.

❖ *You can use rum or any coffee flavoured liqueur instead for the above recipe.*

CHOCOLATE ORANGE CHEESECAKE

Vanilla sponge layered with a delectable chocolate and orange flavoured cheesecake.

Prep. time : 15 mins.   Cooking time : 40 mins.   Makes 1 cake.

For the vanilla sponge
½ cup condensed milk
1¼ cups plain flour (maida)
1 teaspoon baking powder
½ teaspoon soda bi-carb
¼ cup melted butter
1 teaspoon vanilla essence

To be mixed into a soaking syrup
2 tablespoons sugar
½ cup water

For the chocolate orange cheesecake

5 grams agar agar (china grass)

2 cups curds, hung for 30 minutes

zest of 1 orange (optional)

1 tablespoon orange squash

3 tablespoons melted chocolate

½ cup (100 grams) cream

¼ cup powdered sugar

½ teaspoon vanilla essence

For the garnish

orange segments

For the vanilla sponge

1. Sieve the flour, baking powder and soda bi-carb together.
2. Mix the flour mixture, condensed milk, melted butter, vanilla essence and 75 ml. of water in a bowl, using a whisk.
3. Pour this mixture into a greased and dusted 150 mm. (6") diameter tin.
4. Bake in a hot oven at 200°C (400°F) for 10 minutes. Then reduce the temperature to 150°C (300°F) and a bake for a further 15 minutes.
5. The cake is ready when it leaves the sides of the tin and is springy to touch. When ready, remove from the oven and leave for 1 minute. Invert the tin over a rack.
6. Cool the cake.

For the chocolate orange cheesecake

1. Dissolve the agar agar in ¼ cup of water and bring to a boil over gentle heat. Keep warm.
2. In a large bowl, mix together the curds, orange zest, squash, melted chocolate and whisk till it is smooth. Keep aside.
3. In another bowl, whisk the cream, sugar and vanilla essence till soft peaks form.
4. Add the warm agar agar solution into the curds mixture and mix well .
5. Fold in the whipped cream and mix gently.

How to proceed

1. Slice the cake into 2 portions horizontally.
2. Place one slice in a loose bottomed cake tin and sprinkle some soaking syrup.
3. Pour the cheesecake mixture over the sponge.
4. Place the other layer of the sponge on top and soak with the remaining soaking syrup.
5. Refrigerate for 4 hours or till it sets.
6. Unmould and serve chilled, garnished with orange segments.

❖ *When you hang 2 cups of the curds for 30 minutes, you should get about 1 cup of thick curds.*
❖ *If you do not have a loose bottomed tin, cut a 75 mm. (3") thick strip of thick plastic or acetate sheet and line the sides to surround the circumference of the sponge with it.*
Seal the edge using a staple pin.

CHOCOLATE TRUFFLE ICE-CREAM

A rich and creamy frozen dessert.

Prep. time : 5 mins.   Cooking time : 10 mins.   Makes 4 scoops.

½ cup (60 grams) dark chocolate, chopped

2 teaspoons cornflour

1 cup milk

3 tablespoons castor sugar

½ cup (100 grams) fresh cream

1. Heat 2 tablespoons of water in a saucepan and bring to a boil. Remove from the fire, add the dark chocolate and mix well to get a smooth sauce. Keep aside.

2. Mix the cornflour in 1 to 2 tablespoons of cold water and keep aside.

3. Heat the milk in a heavy bottomed pan. When it comes to a boil, add the dissolved cornflour and castor sugar and cook for a further 2 minutes, stirring continuously.

4. Remove from the heat and cool completely.

5. Whip the cream till soft peaks form.

6. Gently fold the cooled milk mixture and the melted chocolate into the whipped cream using a spatula.

7. Pour into a shallow freezer-proof dish and freeze till slushy.

8. Remove from the freezer and beat with a whisk till it is smooth and creamy.

9. Freeze again till firm.

❖ *You can also add white or dark chocolate chips*
into this recipe at step 8, to get
Chocolate Chip Ice-cream.

30

MOCHA MOUSSE CAKE

Picture on page 36

A coffee and chocolate mousse on a muesli base.

Prep. time : 15 mins.   Cooking time : 10 mins.   Makes 1 cake.

For the muesli base
¾ cup crushed cornflakes
¼ cup chopped nuts (almonds, pistachios, walnuts)
¼ cup (30 grams) dark chocolate, grated

For the mocha mousse
5 grams agar agar (china grass)
1½ tablespoons custard powder
½ cup milk
1½ teaspoons instant coffee powder
½ cup (60 grams) dark chocolate, grated
1 cup (200 grams) fresh cream
6 tablespoons powdered sugar
½ teaspoon vanilla essence

For the garnish
dark, milk and white chocolate curls, page 10
½ recipe chocolate sauce, page 87

For the muesli base
1. Melt the chocolate over gentle heat.
2. Combine all the ingredients in a bowl, add the melted chocolate and mix well.
3. Press this mixture evenly onto a 150 mm. (6") diameter loose bottomed cake tin.
4. Refrigerate for 15 to 20 minutes.

For the mocha mousse

1. Dissolve the agar agar in ½ cup (100 ml.) of water and melt over a medium flame till it becomes a smooth solution. Keep warm.
2. Combine the custard powder, milk, coffee powder and chocolate in a bowl and mix well.
3. Bring to a boil, stirring continuously. Simmer for 2 minutes.
4. Combine the agar-agar solution, chocolate custard and mix well.
5. In a another bowl, combine the fresh cream, sugar and vanilla essence and whisk till soft peaks form.
6. Gently mix the whipped cream and chocolate custard and pour over the prepared muesli base.
7. Refrigerate till set.
8. Garnish with chocolate curls and drizzle the chocolate sauce on top.

Serve chilled.

❖ *You can also use readymade Muesli instead of crushed cornflakes and nuts for the above recipe.*
❖ *Serving Suggestion :*
This mousse cake is best served with
a cherry or strawberry sauce as
shown in the picture on page 36.

CHOCOLATE LEMON MOUSSE CAKE

Picture on page 53

Rich chocolate cake topped with a tangy lemon mousse.

Prep. time : 30 mins.   Cooking time : 40 mins.   Makes 1 cake.

For the chocolate cake

½ cup plain flour (maida)

1 tablespoon cocoa powder

2 tablespoons sour curds

¼ teaspoon soda bi-carb

¼ cup melted butter

⅓ cup powdered sugar

½ teaspoon vanilla essence

For the lemon mousse

1 tablespoon cornflour

1 cup milk

4 tablespoons sugar

1 teaspoon lemon rind, grated

juice of 2 lemons

2 to 3 drops lemon
yellow food colouring

5 grams agar agar (china grass)

1 cup (200 grams)
fresh cream, chilled

To be mixed into
a soaking syrup

2 tablespoons sugar

1 teaspoon lemon juice

⅓ cup water

For the garnish

whipped cream

lemon slices

fresh fruits

mint sprigs

For the chocolate cake

1. Sieve the flour and cocoa powder. Keep aside.
2. Mix the curds and soda bi-carb in a bowl and keep aside.
3. Combine the butter, sugar and ¼ cup of hot water in another bowl.

4. Add the flour mixture, curds and vanilla essence and mix to make a smooth batter.
5. Put the mixture in a 200 mm. (8") diameter greased baking tin.
6. Bake in a pre-heated oven at 200°C (400°F) for 30 minutes or until a knife inserted in the cake comes out clean.
7. Remove from the oven and cool.

For lemon mousse

1. Dissolve the cornflour in 3 tablespoons of cold water. Keep aside.
2. Heat the milk, add the dissolved cornflour and sugar and bring to a boil. Cool completely.
3. Add the lemon rind, lemon juice and lemon yellow food colouring to the milk and mix well.
4. Dissolve the agar agar in ½ cup (100 ml.) of water and cook over gentle heat till the agar agar dissolves. Keep warm.
5. Gently whip the cream till soft peaks form and keep refrigerated.
6. Mix the lemon mixture, agar agar and cream together using a spatula.

How to proceed

1. Place the chocolate cake in a 200 mm. (8") diameter loose bottomed cake tin. Sprinkle the soaking syrup over it.
2. Spoon the lemon mousse mixture over it. Refrigerate till the mousse has set completely.
3. Unmould the mousse cake.
4. Garnish with whipped cream, lemon slices, fruits and mint sprigs. Serve chilled.

❖ *If the agar agar has not dissolved evenly,*
strain the mixture before you mix it with the cream
and lemon mixture.

Facing page: Chocolate Mousse, *page 25*.

BLACK FOREST GATEAU

Picture on page 54

A classic German dessert of chocolate sponge layered with cream and cherries.

Prep. time : 15 mins.   Cooking time : 30 mins.   Makes 1 gateau.

1 recipe chocolate cake, page 16

For the Chantilly cream

1¼ cups (250 grams)
fresh cream, chilled

4 tablespoons powdered sugar

1 teaspoon vanilla essence

**To be mixed into
a soaking syrup**

2 tablespoons sugar

2 tablespoons
cherry liqueur (optional)

½ cup water

For the filling

1½ cups cherries, deseeded

For the garnish

dark chocolate curls, page 10

6 cherries, deseeded

¼ cup whipped cream

For the Chantilly cream

1. Whip the cream, sugar and vanilla essence and whisk till soft peaks form.
2. Keep refrigerated till required.

Facing page: Mocha Mousse Cake, *page 31.*

How to proceed

1. Slice the chocolate cake horizontally into 2 equal parts.
2. Soak the bottom layer of the chocolate cake with half the soaking syrup.
3. Spread half the Chantilly cream on the soaked layer of the cake.
4. Place half the cherries on top and sandwich with the second layer of the chocolate cake.
5. Soak with the remaining soaking syrup and spread the remaining Chantilly cream on top.
6. Garnish with the remaining cherries, chocolate curls and whipped cream swirls as shown in the picture on page 54.

❖ *You can also use grated chocolate, page 10 to garnish the cake. Sprinkle it on the sides as well as on the top.*

CHOCOLATE CARROT LOAF

**A moist carrot cake flavoured with chocolate
which melts in the mouth.**

Prep. time : 15 mins.   Cooking time : 50 mins.   Makes 1 loaf.

½ cup melted butter
½ cup condensed milk
2 teaspoons golden syrup
2 tablespoons eastor sugar
¾ cup grated carrot
¾ cup self-raising flour
¼ teaspoon soda bi-carb
2 tablespoons cocoa powder
2 tablespoons walnuts, chopped
2 tablespoons sultanas
1 teaspoon vanilla essence
butter for greasing

For the garnish
1 tablespoon icing sugar

1. Combine all the ingredients in a bowl and mix together into a smooth batter making sure that no lumps remain.
2. Spoon the mixture into a 150 mm. (6") x 100 mm. (4") greased and dusted loaf tin.
3. Bake in a pre-heated oven at 180°C (360°F) for 45 to 50 minutes.
4. Remove from the oven and cool on a wire rack.
5. Sprinkle with the icing sugar and serve warm.

❖ *To test if the loaf is cooked, insert a knife or
a skewer into the loaf. If it is cooked,
the knife will come out clean.*

40

BROWNIE MUFFINS

**Devilish dark chocolate brownies baked
in muffin moulds.**

Prep. time : 10 mins.   Cooking time : 30 mins.   Makes 8 muffins.

1 ⅔ cups (200 grams) dark chocolate, chopped

⅔ cup butter

½ cup condensed milk

¾ cup plain flour (maida)

½ cup chopped walnuts

1 teaspoon vanilla essence

butter for greasing

1. Melt the dark chocolate and butter with 2 tablespoons of water over gentle heat and mix well so that no lumps remain.
2. Remove from the fire, add the condensed milk and mix well. Cool to room temperature.
3. Add the flour, walnuts and vanilla essence and mix well.
4. Spoon 2 tablespoons of the mixture into 8 greased and dusted muffin moulds.
5. Bake in a pre-heated oven at 180°C (360°F) for 20 to 25 minutes or until a knife or skewer inserted into the brownie comes out clean.
6. Cool on a wire rack and unmould each muffin.
    Serve warm.

❖ *Serving suggestion : Serve these with vanilla ice-cream.*

41

CHOCOLATE APPLE RING

Chocolate cake flavoured with apple purée, cinnamon and nutmeg. A blend of subtle flavours.

Prep. time : 15 mins.   Cooking time : 40 mins.   Makes 1 cake.

2 apples
¾ cup plain flour (maida)
5 tablespoons cocoa powder
1 teaspoon baking powder
1½ teaspoons cinnamon powder (dalchini)
¼ teaspoon nutmeg powder (jaiphal)
½ teaspoon salt
3 tablespoons butter, softened
¼ cup powdered sugar
1⅓ cups condensed milk

1. Peel and chop the apples and place them in a saucepan with ½ cup of water.
2. Bring the apples to a boil and simmer for 2 to 3 minutes.
3. Cool and mash to a pulp.
4. Sieve together the flour, cocoa powder, baking powder, cinnamon powder, nutmeg powder and salt.
5. In a bowl, cream the butter and sugar till light and fluffy.
6. Add the condensed milk, flour mixture and mashed apples and mix well.
7. Pour this mixture into a greased 200 mm. (8") diameter ring mould.
8. Bake in a pre-heated oven at 180°C (360°F) for 25 to 30 minutes or until a knife inserted into the cake comes out clean.
9. Cool slightly and unmould the cake.
   Serve warm.

❖ *You can also use this cake batter to make muffins or a large cake.*

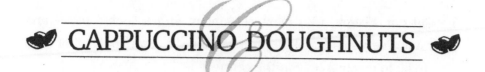 CAPPUCCINO DOUGHNUTS

Picture on cover

Cocoa-cinnamon flavoured doughnuts.

Prep. time : 10 mins.   Cooking time : 15 mins.   Makes 8 doughnuts.

For the doughnuts
1 cup plain flour (maida)

2 teaspoons (10 grams) fresh yeast, crumbled

½ cup milk

3 tablespoons sugar

½ teaspoon salt

½ teaspoon vanilla essence

1 tablespoon butter, softened

To be mixed into a topping
½ cup castor sugar

1 tablespoon cocoa powder

½ teaspoon cinnamon powder
(dalchini)

Other ingredients
oil for frying

For the doughnuts
1. Combine all the ingredients except the butter in a bowl and knead into a soft dough.
2. Add the butter and knead again till the dough is smooth and elastic (approx. 3 to 5 minutes).
3. Cover with a wet muslin cloth and allow it to prove until it doubles in volume (approx. 15 to 20 minutes).
4. Press the dough lightly to remove the air.
5. Roll out the dough into a sheet of 6 mm. (¼") thickness.

6. Cut out 75 mm. (3") diameter circles with a cookie cutter and using a very small cookie cutter, cut out the centre portion of each circle, to create a hole in the centre.

7. Knead the left-over portion of the dough lightly and repeat steps 5 and 6.

8. Cover with a wet muslin cloth till the doughnuts double in volume again (approx. 5 to 10 minutes).

How to proceed

1. Lift carefully and deep fry in hot oil over a medium flame until both sides are golden brown.

2. Drain on absorbent paper and place on a serving plate.

3. Dust the castor sugar mixture generously on top of the doughnuts. Serve immediately.

VARIATION :

CHOCOLATE DOUGHNUTS, *Picture on cover.*

You can also coat the doughnuts with melted chocolate as shown in the picture.

CHOCOLATE BANANA CAKE

An ideal tea-time cake.

Prep. time : 15 mins.   Cooking time : 35 mins.   Makes 1 cake.

1½ cups self-raising flour

2 tablespoons cocoa powder

½ teaspoon soda bi-carb

½ cup melted butter

¾ cup brown sugar

½ cup condensed milk

1 cup ripe bananas, mashed

1 teaspoon vanilla essence

¾ cup (150 grams) cream

butter for greasing

1. Sieve the flour, cocoa powder and soda bi-carb together.
2. In a large bowl, mix the butter, brown sugar, condensed milk, bananas and vanilla essence together.
3. Gradually, add in the flour mixture and the cream and mix to make a smooth batter.
4. Pour the batter into a 200 mm. (8") diameter greased cake tin.
5. Bake in a pre-heated oven at 180°C (360°F) for 30 to 35 minutes or until a knife inserted in the cake comes out clean.
6. Remove from the oven and cool on a wire rack.

CHOCOLATE COCONUT CAKE

**Desiccated coconut and grated chocolate flavour
this easy-to-make tea cake.**

Prep. time : 15 mins.   Cooking time : 30 mins.   Makes 1 cake.

1½ cups plain flour (maida)

¾ teaspoon baking powder

¾ cup butter, softened

¼ cup brown sugar

2 tablespoons golden syrup

¼ cup condensed milk

½ cup desiccated coconut

½ cup (60 grams) dark chocolate, grated

½ cup milk

1 teaspoon vanilla essence

1. Sieve the flour with the baking powder. Keep aside.
2. Cream the butter and brown sugar till light and fluffy.
3. Add the golden syrup and condensed milk and mix well.
4. Add the remaining ingredients and make a smooth batter making sure no lumps remain.
5. Pour into a 200 mm. (8") diameter greased and dusted cake tin.
6. Bake in a pre-heated oven at 180°C (360°F) for 25 to 30 minutes until the cake is golden brown in colour or a knife inserted in the cake comes out clean.
7. Cool on a wire rack.

❖ *Serving Suggestion :*
You can top this cake with melted chocolate
after it has cooled.

46

CHOCOLATE APPLE PIE

A chocolate version of the favourite apple pie.

Prep. time : 10 mins.   Cooking time : 30 mins.   Makes 1 pie.

For the chocolate pastry

¾ cup plain flour (maida)

3 tablespoons cocoa powder

5 tablespoons powdered sugar

4 tablespoons butter, frozen and
cut into small pieces

For the filling

2 apples

2 tablespoons brown sugar

2 tablespoons chopped walnuts

2 tablespoons sultanas

¼ teaspoon cinnamon powder
(dalchini)

For the chocolate pastry

1. Combine all the ingredients in a bowl and rub the butter into the flour using your fingertips till it resembles bread crumbs .

2. Add 1 tablespoon of cold water and gently knead it into a firm dough. Refrigerate for 10 to 15 minutes.

3. Roll out ⅔ of the dough into a circle and line a 150 mm. (6") diameter pie dish as shown in the diagram on page 48.

4. Prick with a fork at regular intervals and refrigerate for 10 minutes.

5. Bake in a pre-heated oven at 180°C (360°F) for 10 minutes and remove from the oven.

6. Roll the remaining dough into a circle of 200 mm. (6") diameter and keep aside.

For the filling

1. Slice the apples thinly.

2. Mix the sugar, walnuts, sultanas and cinnamon powder and keep aside.

How to proceed

1. Place the apple slices on the half baked chocolate pastry and sprinkle the sugar mixture on top.

2. Cover with the remaining rolled out chocolate pastry and seal the edges. Prick the top of the pie with a fork at regular intervals.

3. Bake in a pre-heated oven at 180°C (360°F) for 10 to 15 minutes or till golden brown.

   Serve hot.

❖ *Serving suggestion :*
Serve with whipped cream or vanilla ice-cream.

HOW TO LINE A PIE DISH?

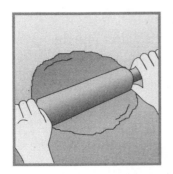

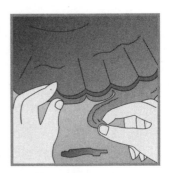

48

CHOCOLATE CHIP APPLE PANCAKES

Delicious pancakes which are so simple to make.

Prep. time : 10 mins.   Cooking time : 10 mins.   Makes 8 pancakes.

1 cup plain flour (maida)

1 apple, peeled and grated

¼ cup (30 grams) dark chocolate, chopped

¾ cup milk

2 tablespoons castor sugar

½ teaspoon vanilla essence

¾ teaspoon baking powder

1 tablespoon melted butter

Other ingredients

butter to cook

honey to serve

1. Combine all the ingredients in a bowl and whisk well to make a smooth batter, making sure no lumps remain. Keep aside.

2. Heat a non-stick pan and spread about 3 to 4 tablespoons of the batter (¼ cup) to make a thick pancake of about 100 mm. (4") diameter.

3. Using a little butter, cook the pancake on both sides over medium heat until golden brown.

4. Repeat the same for the remaining batter to make 7 more pancakes. Serve hot with honey.

CHOCOLATE CHEESE TART

A baked chocolate cheesecake which is light and creamy

Prep. time : 30 mins.   Cooking time : 45 mins.   Makes 1 tart.

For the pastry base

½ cup plain flour (maida)

½ cup butter, softened

2 tablespoons castor sugar

1 tablespoon milk

To be mixed into a filling

1 recipe cream cheese, page 86

½ cup condensed milk

½ cup (60 grams)
dark chocolate, grated

¼ cup sultanas

¼ teaspoon nutmeg powder
(jaiphal)

a pinch soda bi-carb

For the pastry base

1. Sieve the flour.
2. Cream the butter and sugar in a bowl till light and fluffy.
3. Mix in the flour and milk and knead to make a soft dough.
4. Roll out the pastry dough to line the base of a 150 mm. (6") diameter pie dish as shown in the diagram on page 48. Prick the pastry with a fork at regular intervals.
5. Bake in a pre-heated oven at 180°C (360°F) for 15 to 20 minutes.
6. Remove from the oven.

How to proceed

1. Spoon the filling on top of the baked pastry base.
2. Bake in a pre-heated oven at 200°C (400°F) for 20 to 25 minutes or until it is golden brown in colour.
3. Cut into wedges.
   Serve hot.

CHOCOLATE WALNUT TART

Picture on page 54.

Crisp pastry topped with dates, walnuts and chocolate.
Rich, nutritious and divine.

Prep. time : 20 mins.   Cooking time : 45 mins.   Serves 4 to 6.

1 baked pastry base, page 21

For the date filling

½ cup dates, deseeded and
finely chopped

2 teaspoons brandy

1 teaspoon orange rind, grated

To be mixed into a topping

2 tablespoons plain flour (maida)

2 tablespoons castor sugar

2 tablespoons melted butter

¼ cup (30 grams)
dark chocolate, chopped

¼ cup walnuts, chopped

3 tablespoons condensed milk

For the milk chocolate sauce

½ cup (60 grams)
milk chocolate, chopped

¼ cup (50 grams) cream

For the garnish

8 to 10 walnut halves

whipped cream

For the filling

Blend the ingredients for the filling in a food processor.
Keep aside.

51

For the milk chocolate sauce

1. Put the cream in a saucepan and bring to a boil.
2. Remove from the fire, add the milk chocolate and mix well to get a smooth sauce. Cool completely and keep aside.

How to proceed

1. Spread the date filling mixture on top of the baked pastry base.
2. Cover with the topping.
3. Bake in a pre-heated oven at 180°C (360°F) for 15 to 20 minutes or until the tart is golden brown. Cool completely.
4. Top the tart with the milk chocolate sauce.
5. Garnish with the walnut halves and whipped cream.
6. Cut into wedges.
   Serve warm.

❖ *Instead of dates, you can also use dried figs soaked in water for 15 minutes.*

Facing page: Chocolate Lemon Mousse Cake, *page 33*.

STEAMED CHOCOLATE PUDDING

**A rich, warm steamed dessert which
can be made without an oven.**

Prep. time : 20 mins.   Cooking time : 15 mins.   Serves 4 to 6.

1¼ cups (150 grams) dark chocolate, chopped

½ cup milk

1 cup fresh bread crumbs

2 tablespoons butter, softened

1 tablespoon powdered sugar

½ cup condensed milk

½ teaspoon vanilla essence

¼ cup walnuts, chopped

1. Melt the dark chocolate and milk over gentle heat and mix well so that no lumps remain.
2. Add the bread crumbs to it. Mix well and keep aside.
3. Cream the butter and sugar in a bowl till light and fluffy.
4. Add the condensed milk, vanilla essence, walnuts and dark chocolate mixture and mix well.
5. Pour this into a 150 mm. (6") diameter greased cake tin.
6. Cover the cake tin with aluminium foil.
7. Put the cake tin in a pressure cooker and pressure cook for 2 whistles.
8. Unmould, cut into wedges and serve hot.

❖ *To make fresh bread crumbs,
remove the crust of the bread slices and
process it in a dry grinder.*

❶ Chocolate Walnut Tart, *page 51.*
❷ White Chocolate Pistachio Pie, *page 23.*
❸ Black Forest Gateâu, *page 37.*

55

SPICED WALNUT RING

**A walnut cake spiced with nutmeg, cinnamon and ginger,
served topped with chocolate sauce.**

Prep. time : 10 mins.   Cooking time : 30 mins.   Makes 1 ring.

1 cup plain flour (maida)

½ teaspoon baking powder

¼ teaspoon ginger powder (soonth)

¼ teaspoon nutmeg powder (jaiphal)

½ teaspoon cinnamon powder (dalchini)

½ cup butter, softened

¼ cup brown sugar

¼ cup condensed milk

⅓ cup milk

¼ cup walnuts, chopped

To serve

1 recipe chocolate sauce, page 87

1. Sieve the flour with the baking powder, ginger powder, nutmeg powder and cinnamon powder.
2. Cream the butter and brown sugar in a bowl till light and fluffy.
3. Add the condensed milk, flour mixture, milk and walnuts and mix well.
4. Pour this mixture into a greased 125 mm. (5") diameter ring mould.
5. Bake in a pre-heated oven at 180°C (360°F) for 25 to 30 minutes or until a knife inserted into the cake comes out clean.

   Serve warm drizzled with chocolate sauce.

Cookies & Slices

CHOCOLATE COOKIES

A simple way to make delicious chocolate cookies. An all time favourite recipe for your cookie jar.

Prep. time : 20 mins.   Cooking time : 20 mins.   Makes 20 cookies.

1 cup (125 grams) dark chocolate, grated
1¼ cups self-raising flour
⅓ cup milk powder
¾ cup butter, softened
2 tablespoons castor sugar
¼ cup condensed milk

1. Melt the chocolate over gentle heat and keep aside.
2. Sieve the flour. Combine the flour with the milk powder and keep aside.
3. Cream the butter and castor sugar till light and fluffy.
4. Add the condensed milk and melted chocolate to the butter and sugar mixture and mix well.
5. Fold in the flour mixture and mix to form a soft dough.
6. Refrigerate the dough for about 20 minutes.
7. Divide the dough into 20 equal portions and shape into round cookies.
8. Place the cookies on a greased baking tray.
9. Bake in a pre-heated oven at 160°C (320°F) for about 15 to 20 minutes.
10. Remove from the baking tray and cool on a wire rack.
11. Store in an air-tight container.

VARIATION :
CHOCOLATE CHOCOLATE CHIP COOKIES, *Picture on page 71.*
Add ½ cup (60 grams) dark chocolate, chopped, at step 5 along with the flour.

58

WALNUT GANACHE COOKIES

Picture on page 71

**Delicious butter cookies layered with
a chocolate walnut ganache.**

Prep. time : 10 mins.   Cooking time : 35 mins.   Makes 12 cookies.

For the walnut ganache

½ cup (60 grams)
dark chocolate, grated

1 tablespoon cream

3 tablespoons powdered walnuts

For the cookie dough

½ cup plain flour (maida)

2 tablespoons sugar

2 tablespoons butter, frozen
and cut into small pieces

¼ teaspoon vanilla essence

For the walnut ganache

Combine all the ingredients in a saucepan and melt over gentle heat
to get a smooth mixture.

For the cookie dough

1. Combine all the ingredients in a bowl and rub the butter into the
    flour using your fingertips till it resembles bread crumbs.
2. Add 1 teaspoon of water and knead gently into a firm dough.
3. Refrigerate for about 10 to 15 minutes.
4. Roll out the dough into a square of 150 mm. x 150 mm. (6" x 6")
    and 5 mm. (1/5") in thickness.
5. Cut the rolled dough into 3 strips of 50 mm. (2") width. Keep
    aside.

How to proceed

1. Place one cookie dough strip on a dry surface and spread a layer of
    the walnut ganache on top.
2. Top with the second cookie dough strip and spread another layer
    of the walnut ganache.

59

3. Top with the third cookie dough strip.

4. Refrigerate for at least 30 minutes till the layers are firm.

5. Cut horizontally into slices of 12 mm. (½") thickness and place them on a baking tray.

6. Bake in a pre-heated oven at 180°C (360°F) for 20 to 25 minutes.

7. Cool completely and store in air-tight containers.

❧ CHOCOLATE CHIP COOKIES ❧

Picture on page 71

Rice flour adds more crispiness to this cookie dough.

Prep. time : 10 mins.   Cooking time : 30 mins.   Makes 9 cookies.

¾ cup butter, softened

3 tablespoons sugar

½ teaspoon vanilla essence

1 cup plain flour (maida)

2 tablespoons rice flour

½ cup (60 grams) dark chocolate, chopped

1. Cream the butter, sugar and vanilla essence in a bowl till light and fluffy.

2. Add the flour and rice flour and mix well.

3. Fold in the chocolate to form a soft dough. Divide the dough into 9 equal portions.

4. Roll each portion into a ball and flatten using your palm.

5. Place the cookies on a baking tray and bake in a pre-heated oven at 160°C (320°F) for 25 to 30 minutes till they are golden brown.

6. Cool completely and store in an air-tight container.

❖ *Double the recipe to make more cookies and store for unexpected guests.*

60

HARLEQUIN COOKIES

Picture on page 71

A simple way to make delicious butter cookies dipped in dark chocolate.

Prep. time : 20 mins.   Cooking time : 20 mins.   Makes 20 cookies.

1¼ cups self-raising flour

⅓ cup milk powder

¾ cup butter, softened

2 tablespoons castor sugar

¼ cup condensed milk

½ recipe tempered chocolate, page 70.

1. Sieve the flour. Combine the flour with the milk powder and keep aside.
2. Cream the butter and castor sugar till light and fluffy.
3. Add the condensed milk to the butter and sugar and mix well.
4. Fold in the flour mixture to form a soft dough.
5. Refrigerate the dough for about 20 minutes.
6. Divide the dough into 20 equal portions and shape into round cookies or cut using a cookie cutter.
7. Place the cookies on a greased baking tray.
8. Bake in a pre-heated oven at 160°C (320°F) for about 15 to 20 minutes.
9. Remove from the baking tray and cool on a wire rack.
10. Dip half of each cookie into the tempered chocolate and allow to set on a wire rack as shown in the picture on page 71.

CHOCOLATE FILLED SHORTBREADS

Picture on page 71

Shortbreads with a scrumptious chocolate cheese filling.
Prep. time : 20 mins. Cooking time : 30 mins. Makes 18-20 shortbreads

For the shortbread dough
1 cup plain flour (maida)
¼ teaspoon baking powder
½ cup cornflour
¾ cup icing sugar
¾ cup butter, softened

For the filling
¼ cup (30 grams)
dark chocolate, grated
¼ cup cottage
cheese (paneer), grated
1 teaspoon orange
squash (optional)

For the garnish
2 tablespoons cocoa powder

For the shortbread dough
1. Sieve together the flour, baking powder and cornflour. Keep aside.
2. Cream the icing sugar and butter till light and fluffy.
3. Add the flour mixture and mix well to make a soft dough. Refrigerate for about 15 minutes.

For the filling
Combine all the ingredients and divide into 18 to 20 portions. Keep aside.

How to proceed
1. Divide the dough into 2 portions and roll out each portion into a sheet of 3 mm. (⅛") thickness.
2. Brush one sheet with cold water and place portions of the filling on it at an equal distance from each other.

3. Cover with the second sheet and press down around each mound of filling.

4. Cut into circles using a 75 mm. (3") diameter cookie cutter, ensuring that the filling stays in the centre.

5. Knead the left-over portion of the dough and repeat steps 1 to 4.

6. Place the cookies on a greased baking tray and bake in a pre-heated oven at 180°C (360°F) for 10 to 15 minutes.

7. Remove from the oven and cool on a wire rack.

8. Using a sieve, dust the cookies with cocoa powder.

9. Store in an air-tight container.

 # NO FUSS BROWNIES

Picture on cover

Creamy chocolate enriched with walnuts, almonds and biscuits. You do not have to bake these delicious treats.
Prep. time : 5 mins.   Cooking time : 7 mins.   Makes 1 cake.

¾ cup (90 grams) dark chocolate, chopped
½ cup butter
¾ cup crushed digestive biscuits
¼ cup condensed milk
½ cup (80 grams) mixed nuts (walnuts, almonds, cashewnuts),
chopped
butter for greasing

For the garnish
slivered almonds
whipped cream mixed with chocolate sauce, page 87

1. Grease a 150 mm. x 150 mm. (6" x 6") square cake tin.

2. Combine the chocolate and butter in a bowl and melt over a double boiler till it becomes a smooth sauce.

3. Remove from the fire, add the remaining ingredients and mix well.

4. Pour into the greased tin and refrigerate till set.

5. Cut into wedges.

6. Garnish with slivered almonds and pipe out swirls of the cream and chocolate sauce mixture.
   Serve chilled.

❖ *Use blanched and skinned almonds for the above recipe.*
❖ *You can also cut these using round and hexagonal shaped cookie cutters as shown in the picture on cover.*

 # TRUFFLE NUT CAKE

An unbelievably rich chocolate nut cake. Marmalade adds that special tang to this dessert.

Prep. time : 15 mins.   Cooking time : 45 mins.   Makes 1 cake.

1¼ cups (150 grams) grated dark chocolate, tightly packed

2 tablespoons honey

¼ cup orange marmalade

2 tablespoons butter

½ cup almonds, chopped

½ cup walnuts, chopped

½ cup sultanas

¾ cup grated coconut

¼ cup plain flour (maida)

1 teaspoon cinnamon powder (dalchini)

1. Combine the chocolate, honey, marmalade and butter in a saucepan.

2. Melt over gentle heat till it becomes a smooth sauce.

3. Remove from the fire, add the remaining ingredients and mix well.
   Pour into a greased 200 mm. (8") diameter baking tin.

4. Bake in a pre-heated oven at 160°C (320°F) for 35 minutes or until a knife inserted in the cake comes out clean.

5. Remove from the oven and cool slightly.
   Serve warm with coffee.

 CHOCOLATE WALNUT SLICE

A crisp chocolate walnut slice that melts in the mouth.

Prep. time : 10 mins.   Cooking time : 25 mins.   Makes 18 pieces.

½ cup plain flour (maida)

¼ teaspoon soda bi-carb

⅓ cup coarsely powdered walnuts

2 tablespoons castor sugar

2 tablespoons golden syrup

¼ cup (30 grams) dark chocolate, grated

¼ cup condensed milk

⅓ cup melted butter

1. Sieve the flour with the soda bi-carb. Add the walnut powder and castor sugar and keep aside.

2. Heat the golden syrup, dark chocolate and condensed milk in a non-stick pan over gentle heat. Keep aside.

3. Combine together the chocolate mixture, flour mixture and melted butter and mix well.

4. Pour into a greased 150 mm. x 150 mm. (6" x 6") square baking tin.

5. Bake in a pre-heated oven at 180°C (360°F) for about 20 minutes or until a knife inserted in the slice comes out clean. .

6. Cool slightly, unmould and cut into 50 mm. x 25 mm. (2" x 1") pieces, while it is still warm.

7. Store in an air-tight container.

CHUNKY CHOCOLATE AND PEANUT COOKIES

Picture on page 71

Orange flavoured cookies made with whole wheat flour, oats, peanuts, chocolate chips and coconut.

Prep. time : 10 mins. Cooking time : 20 mins. Makes 2 large cookies.

⅓ cup butter

3 tablespoons brown sugar

⅓ cup whole wheat flour (gehun ka atta)

3 tablespoons rolled oats

⅓ cup (40 grams) dark chocolate, chopped

1 tablespoon roasted unsalted peanuts, chopped

1 tablespoon orange squash

½ teaspoon grated orange rind (optional)

3 tablespoons desiccated coconut

1. Cream the butter and sugar till light and fluffy.
2. Add the whole wheat flour, oats, dark chocolate, peanuts, orange squash, orange rind and desiccated coconut. Mix well.
3. Divide the mixture into two equal portions.
4. Press onto a greased baking tray to make 100 mm. (4") diameter circles.
5. Bake in a pre-heated oven at 160 °C (320°F) for 20 minutes or until evenly browned. Cool completely.
6. Store in an air-tight container.

❖ *You can drizzle melted white chocolate over the cookies as shown in the picture on page 71 after they are cool.*

LEMON POLKA DOT COOKIES

Picture on page 71

Lemon flavoured cookie dough baked and dotted with melted chocolate.

Prep. time : 20 mins.   Cooking time : 20 mins.   Makes 20 cookies.

For the lemon cookies

1¼ cups self-raising flour

⅓ cup milk powder

¾ cup butter, softened

2 tablespoons castor sugar

¼ cup condensed milk

1 teaspoon lemon rind, grated

For the polka dots

½ cup (60 grams) chocolate, grated

For the lemon cookies

1. Sieve the flour. Combine the flour with the milk powder and keep aside.
2. Cream the butter and castor sugar till light and fluffy.
3. Add the condensed milk and lemon rind to the butter and sugar and mix well.
4. Fold in the flour mixture and mix to form a soft dough.
5. Refrigerate the dough for about 20 minutes.
6. Divide the dough into 20 equal portions and shape into round cookies.
7. Place the cookies on a greased baking tray.
8. Bake in a pre-heated oven at 160°C (320°F) for about 15 to 20 minutes.
9. Remove from the baking tray and cool on a wire rack.

How to proceed

1. Melt the chocolate over a double boiler and cool slightly.
2. Pour into a piping bag and pipe dots on each cookie.
3. Allow it to set and store in an air-tight container.

CHOCOLATE WALNUT FUDGE

**A rich chocolate walnut fudge. Great to serve
with a glass of milk.**

Prep. time : 5 mins.   Cooking time : 15 mins.   Serves 4.

½ can (400 grams for full can) condensed milk

⅓ cup cocoa powder

½ teaspoon vanilla essence

1 tablespoon plain flour (maida)

½ cup (60 grams) butter

½ cup chopped walnuts

Other ingredients

oil for greasing

1. Combine all the ingredients except the walnuts in a heavy bottomed saucepan and cook over a medium flame, stirring continuously.
2. Cook till the mixture thickens and starts leaving the sides of the pan (approx. 10 minutes).
3. Add the walnuts and mix well.
4. Put into a tin 100 mm. x 100 mm. (4" x 4") greased square tin and allow it to set at room temperature.
5. Cut into squares and store in an air-tight container.

❖ *You can use cashewnuts instead of walnuts.*

68

Chocolate Making

HOW TO TEMPER CHOCOLATE

This method of melting chocolate and then cooling it to room temperature is called TEMPERING.

Prep. time : 5 mins.   Cooking time : 10 mins.   Makes 2 cups.

250 grams chocolate (dark, milk or white)

1. Chop the chocolate into small even-sized pieces and put it in a bowl.

2. Place the bowl on top of a double boiler as shown in the diagram, taking care to see that the base of the bowl is not in contact with the water in the double boiler.

3. Once the chocolate starts melting, stir continuously till the chocolate melts completely and resembles a smooth sauce [about 42°C (108°F)].

4. Immediately remove from the double boiler and pour onto a clean, dry marble surface or your kitchen platform.

5. Cool the chocolate to room temperature using a palette knife by using the flat side in an up and down motion, so that the chocolate cools evenly and no lumps remain [approx. 26°C (80°F)].

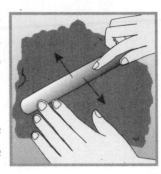

6. At room temperature, the chocolate will neither be warm nor cool. To test the temperature of the chocolate, touch it with the back of your finger.

7. Put the chocolate back into the bowl with the help of your palette knife or dough cutter.

   Use this melted chocolate immediately, as required in the recipe.

GOLDEN RULES OF CHOCOLATE TEMPERING

❖ Do not over-heat chocolate since when overcooked, the chocolate turns from a glossy, liquid mass to a dull, coarse textured mass in which case, the chocolate will have to be discarded.

❖ The chocolate will thicken while you are working on it. If this happens, melt it again on the double boiler, taking care to see it does not burn.

❖ Ensure that the water from the base of the pan does not come in contact with the chocolate.

VARIATION :

MOULDED TEMPERED CHOCOLATES, *Picture on facing page.*
You can put tempered chocolate in the chocolate mould, tap it gently and clean the upper surface of the chocolate mould using a palette knife. Refrigerate till the chocolates have set and then upturn the mould lightly to unmould the chocolates.

❶ Maltese Truffles, *page 81.*
❷ White Chocolate Praline Rocks, *page 75.*
❸ White Chocolate Pistachio Truffles, *page 74.*
❹ Coffee Truffles, *page 82.*
❺ Rum Centred Chocolates, *page 77.*
❻ Moulded Tempered Chocolates, *above.*

73

WHITE CHOCOLATE PISTACHIO TRUFFLES

Picture on page 72

These delicious creamy white chocolate truffles will testify that nothing is as nice as home-made chocolates.

Prep. time : 10 mins.   Cooking time : 5 mins.   Makes 30 truffles.

For the white chocolate truffle

1 cup (125 grams) white chocolate, chopped

$\frac{1}{3}$ cup fresh cream

a few drops coconut essence

To be mixed into a topping

3 tablespoons coarsely powdered pistachios

3 tablespoons desiccated coconut

For the white chocolate truffle

1. Heat the cream in a broad pan and bring it to a boil.
2. Remove from the fire and add the white chocolate and coconut essence. Mix well to get a smooth mixture.
3. Refrigerate until firm.

How to proceed

1. Divide the white chocolate truffle into 30 equal portions.
2. Shape into even sized rounds.
3. Evenly coat the pistachio and coconut topping on the truffles by rolling them in the topping mixture.
4. Refrigerate until firm.
    Serve chilled.

❖ *Use 1 tablespoon Malibu (coconut flavoured liqueur) instead of coconut essence to get a better flavour.*

WHITE CHOCOLATE PRALINE ROCKS

Picture on page 72

Crisp walnut praline encased in rich white chocolate is tempting to nibble at any time of the day.

Prep. time : 5 mins. Cooking time : 15 mins. Makes approx. 25 rocks.

For the walnut praline
⅓ cup sugar

½ cup walnuts, chopped

oil for greasing

1 recipe tempered white chocolate, page 70

For the garnish (optional)
¼ recipe tempered dark chocolate, page 70

For the walnut praline

1. Heat the sugar in a heavy bottomed pan while stirring continuously till it caramelises to a light brown colour and the sugar melts completely.
2. Remove from the fire, add the walnuts and mix well.
3. Pour onto a greased marble or stone surface, flatten a little using a greased palette knife and allow it to cool and harden completely.
4. Crush into pieces using a heavy rolling pin. Keep aside.

How to proceed

1. Add the walnut praline to the tempered white chocolate and mix well.
2. Drop tablespoonfuls of this mixture on a tray lined with grease-proof paper or foil and refrigerate till the rocks are firm.

3. Garnish the rocks with streaks of tempered dark chocolate as shown in the picture on page 72.
4. Allow to set.
5. Store refrigerated in an air-tight container.

❖ *You can use any dry fruit of your choice instead of the walnuts.*

 # PEANUT BUTTER BITES

A sumptuous mixture of peanut butter and cocoa powder coated with rich dark chocolate. These will be a favourite with adults and children alike.

Prep. time : 5 mins.   No cooking.   Makes 15 pieces.

½ recipe tempered dark chocolate, page 70

For the filling

1 cup peanut butter

⅓ cup icing sugar

¼ cup cocoa powder

1. Combine the peanut butter, icing sugar and cocoa powder in a bowl. Mix well.
2. Divide into 15 equal portions and shape each portion into even sized rounds. Keep aside.
3. Dip each portion in the tempered chocolate and lift it out with a fork.
4. Tap off all the excess chocolate and place on a tray lined with grease-proof paper or foil.
5. Refrigerate for about 10 minutes or until set.
6. Store refrigerated in air-tight containers.

RUM CENTRED CHOCOLATES

Picture on page 72

Moulded chocolates with a rum and icing sugar filling.

Prep. time : 10 mins.   Cooking time : 10 mins.   Makes 12 chocolates.

For the rum filling
½ cup icing sugar
1 tablespoon rum

For the chocolate covering
250 grams dark chocolate

For the rum filling

Mix the icing sugar and rum very well until no lumps remain.

Keep aside.

For the chocolate covering

1. Chop the chocolate into small even-sized pieces and put it in a bowl.

2. Place the bowl on top of a double boiler, as shown in the diagram on page 7, taking care to see that the base of the bowl is not in contact with the water in the double boiler.

3. Once the chocolate starts melting, stir continuously till the chocolate melts completely and resembles a smooth sauce [(about 42°C (108°F)].

4. Immediately remove from the double boiler and pour onto a clean, dry marble surface or your kitchen platform.

5. Cool the chocolate to room temperature using a palette knife by using the flat side in an up and down motion , so that the chocolate cools evenly and no lumps remain [approx. 26°C (80°F)].

6. At room temperature, the chocolate will neither be warm nor cool. To test the temperature of the chocolate, touch it with the back of your finger.

7. Put the chocolate back into the bowl with the help of your palette knife or dough cutter.

    Use this melted chocolate immediately.

How to proceed

1. Fill the depressions in the chocolate mould with melted chocolate using a tablespoon and tap the chocolate filled mould gently so that the chocolate coats the depressions evenly and no air gaps remain. It is advisable to use chocolate moulds which have depressions of about 12 mm. (½") depth.

 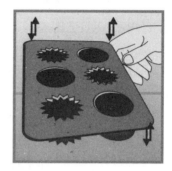

2. Overturn the mould and tap it lightly on your kitchen platform or marble surface at a 45° angle so that all the excess chocolate gets poured out and only a thin layer of chocolate coating the depressions of the mould (i.e. the chocolate shell) remains.

3. Clean the upper surface of the chocolate mould using a palette knife or dough cutter across the chocolate mould.
4. Refrigerate the filled mould for about 10 minutes.
5. Meanwhile put the remaining chocolate back into the bowl with the help of your palette knife or dough cutter. Keep aside.

6. Spoon the rum filling mixture into 12 chocolate shells so that it fills half of each shell.

7. Clean the edges of the mould again with your palette knife or dough-cutter and refrigerate for 15 more minutes.

8. Meanwhile melt the remaining chocolate again repeat the steps **for the chocolate covering (Steps 2 to 7).**

9. Remove the mould from the refrigerator and put 1 teaspoon of the melted chocolate on each chocolate shell. Tap the mould lightly on your work table so as to smoothen the upper surface and to ensure that the chocolate completely covers the filling mixture taking care to see that the rum filling mixture and chocolate do not mix.

10. Clean the edges of each shell using your palette knife or dough cutter.

11. For the final finish, put a little chocolate to cover any air gaps and on places where the filling is visible.
12. Refrigerate till the chocolates have set (approx. 20 to 30 minutes).
13. Upturn the mould and tap lightly to unmould the chocolates. Store refrigerated.

❖ *Take care to see that the stone surface / marble slab and the mould are absolutely dry before you proceed to make the chocolates.*
❖ *If you want to use the mould again immediately, do not wash, but wipe it with cotton and use again.*

Picture on page 72

Candied orange peel centred in a chocolate cases. These are great with coffee after a meal.

Prep. time : 10 mins.   Cooking time : 10 mins.   Makes 15 truffles.

peel of 1 orange, with the white pith removed
4 tablespoons sugar
¼ recipe tempered dark chocolate, page 70

1. Cut the orange peel into small pieces.
2. Blanch these pieces in hot water for about 2 minutes. Drain.
3. Add the sugar to ¾ cup of water and make a sugar syrup of one string consistency.
4. Add the orange peel pieces in it and simmer for about 5 minutes.
5. Drain onto grease-proof paper and allow it to dry for about 30 minutes.
6. Mix the orange peel pieces and tempered chocolate. Fill the depressions in the chocolate mould with this chocolate. Tap the chocolate filled mould gently on your kitchen platform so that the chocolate coats the depressions evenly and no air gaps remain. It is advisable to use chocolate moulds which have depressions of about 12 mm. (½") depth.
7. Tap the moulds lightly to remove the air gaps and scrape off the excess chocolate on top of the moulds using a palette knife across the mould and smoothen the edges.
8. Allow to set in the refrigerator for about 15 minutes.
9. Unmould and store refrigerated in air-tight containers.

COFFEE TRUFFLES

Picture on page 72

These coffee centred morsels are simplicity itself to make. The perfect way to end a meal.

Prep. time : 10 mins.   Cooking time : 10 mins.   Makes 15 truffles.

For the coffee truffle
1 cup (125 grams) milk chocolate, finely chopped
½ cup (100 grams) cream
2 teaspoons instant coffee powder

For the chocolate covering
250 grams dark chocolate

For the coffee truffle
1. Heat the cream in a non-stick pan and bring it to a boil.
2. Remove from the fire, add the coffee powder and chocolate and mix well to get a smooth mixture.
3. Refrigerate till it sets (approx. 30 to 40 minutes).
4. Divide into 15 equal parts and shape into even sized rounds.
5. Refrigerate for another 20 minutes.

For the chocolate covering
1. Chop the chocolate into small even-sized pieces and put it in a bowl.
2. Place the bowl on top of a double boiler as shown in the diagram on page 7, taking care to see that the base of the bowl is not in contact with the water in the double boiler.
3. Once the chocolate starts melting, stir continuously till the chocolate melts completely and resembles a smooth sauce [(about 42°C (108°F)].

4. Immediately remove from the double boiler and pour onto a clean, dry marble surface or your kitchen platform.

5. Cool the chocolate to room temperature using a palette knife by using the flat side in an up and down motion , so that the chocolate cools evenly and no lumps remain [approx. 26°C (80°F)].

6. At room temperature, the chocolate will neither be warm nor cool. To test the temperature of the chocolate, touch it with the back of your finger.

7. Put the chocolate back into the bowl with the help of your palette knife or dough cutter.
   Use this melted chocolate immediately.

How to proceed

1. Fill the depressions in the chocolate mould with melted chocolate using a tablespoon and tap the chocolate filled mould gently so that the chocolate coats the depressions evenly and no air gaps remain. It is advisable to use chocolate moulds which have depressions of about 12 mm. (½") depth.

2. Overturn the mould and tap it lightly on your kitchen platform or a marble surface so that all the excess chocolate gets poured out and only a thin layer of chocolate coating the depressions of the mould (i.e. the chocolate shell) remains.

3. Clean the upper surface of the chocolate mould using a palette knife or dough cutter.

4. Refrigerate the filled mould for about 10 minutes.

5. Meanwhile put the remaining chocolate back into the bowl with the help of your palette knife or dough cutter. Keep aside.

6. Remove the filling mixture from the refrigerator and mix it well, so that no lumps remain.

7. Spoon the filling mixture into each chocolate shell so that it fills half of each shell.

8. Clean the edges of the mould again with your palette knife or dough-cutter and refrigerate for 15 more minutes.

9. Meanwhile melt the remaining chocolate again repeat the steps **for the chocolate covering (Steps 2 to 7).**

10. Remove the mould from the refrigerator and put 1 teaspoon of the melted chocolate on each chocolate shell. Tap the mould lightly on your work table so as to smoothen the upper surface and to ensure that the chocolate completely covers the filling mixture taking care to see that the coffee truffle mixture and chocolate do not mix.

11. Clean the edges of each shell using your palette knife or dough cutter.

12. For the final finish, put a little chocolate to cover any air gaps and on places where the filling is visible.

13. Refrigerate till the chocolates have set (approx. 20 to 30 minutes).

14. Upturn the mould and tap lightly to unmould the chocolates. Store refrigerated.

❖ *You add any liqueur of your choice instead of the coffee powder.*

Basic Recipes

CREAM CHEESE

Prep. time : a few mins.   Cooking time : 10 mins.

Makes 1½ cups (approx.)

1 litre full fat milk

1 teaspoon citric acid crystals

½ cup warm water

1. Put the milk to boil in a thick bottomed pan.
2. When it comes to a boil, remove from the flame and keep aside for a few minutes.
3. In another bowl, mix the citric acid crystals with the warm water.
4. Pour this mixture into the hot milk and allow it to stand for about 5 minutes till the milk curdles on its own and the whey is a clear liquid. Stir gently if required.
5. Strain this mixture using a muslin cloth.
6. Blend the drained milk solids in a food processor till thick and creamy.

    Use as required.

❖ *If the drained whey is milky, heat the milk*
a little more and strain the separated milk solids.

CHOCOLATE SAUCE

Prep. time : 5 mins.　　Cooking time : 10 mins.　　Serves 4.

1 cup (200 grams) fresh cream
1¾ cups (225 grams) dark chocolate, chopped
1 teaspoon butter

1. Heat the cream in a saucepan and bring it to a boil.
2. Remove from the fire, add the chopped chocolate and butter and mix well to get a smooth sauce.
3. Strain the sauce to remove any lumps.
4. Store refrigerated and use as required.

 CHOCOLATE BUTTER CREAM

An easy-to-make and inexpensive chocolate icing.

Preparation time : 5 mins.   No cooking.

Makes 2 cups approximately.

---

1 cup icing margarine

1¼ cups icing sugar

½ cup cocoa powder

¼ teaspoon vanilla essence

1. Sieve the icing sugar and cocoa powder together and keep aside.
2. In a bowl, cream the icing margarine using a wooden spoon till it is light and smooth.
3. Gradually, add the sieved icing sugar and cocoa powder mixture and cream till all the icing sugar is added.
4. Add the vanilla essence and mix well.

You can use this butter cream to ice and decorate any cake.